Copyright © 2019 Tekkan
Artwork Copyright © 2019

All rights reserved.
First Printing, 2019
ISBN 978-1-7343510-0-2

To contact Tekkan please email:
buddhaboy1289@gmail.com

Table of Contents

Transitions . . . . Page 84

Snap Shots . . . . Page 93

How to Read My Poems

I have married the sonnet to the tanka. I tell a story in the sonnet — using three quatrains, separated by line spaces, and a final couplet. The story builds to a conclusion in the couplet. The tanka is a commentary, or a counterpoint, to the sonnet — the combined poems have two endings.

I don't rhyme my sonnets, because I want freer expression. I want to be direct in my meaning — I want people to clearly understand my meaning. The metaphors are inspired by Shakespeare, and the (aimed-for) precision is in imitation of Japanese style. Using the sonnet with the tanka, I am mixing the sensibility of the Occident and the Orient — which I have done by living in England, Japan, and America.

I don't punctuate much in my poetry. I want the words themselves to do the work. There is logic between words, and the forms provide structure. By not using punctuation I hope to direct readers to carefully attend to each word — to appreciate the graininess of words.

Reading my poems silently, say, on a bus, a train, or an airplane, and reading them aloud, may be different experiences. The way I've written there's not always a pause intended at the end of the line. Hint: *My poems are to be recited not as lines, but as phrases, and a phrase often overflows the break at the end of a line. I pause and take a breath where it seems natural for me to pause. Another person may pause differently than I do.*

Each single poem is a piece of a mosaic, and it is my hope that the collection of poems form an accurate portrait of consciousness.

My daughter, Jocelyn MacDonald, is a wonderful artist. Her art work graces this book.

I am Barry MacDonald. I received the *dharma* name, *Tekkan*, which means, Iron Man, a settled practitioner of great determination.

— *Tekkan*

Everyday Mind X

A thaw melted
almost all the snow
except for the piles
the city plows left
along the streets.

The wind chill is way below zero and
I'm walking to my car without mittens
After talking inside a warm room with
My friends — and a friend and I are blabbing

About the supposition that there was
No time or space before the big bang that
Created the cosmos and one pundit
Says because there was no place to stand and

No time to allow it therefore God can
Not exist and there is no afterlife —
And we are strolling outside and the bones
Of my hands are cold as I'm saying just

Because the supposition may be true
Depressing conclusions need not follow.

With freezing hands
there's no time to stand
in the cold and to ponder
indeterminate
facts.

There are days that begin with trouble and
The missteps continue like on Tuesday when
I found the cat vomit by the toilet
And cat poop on the carpet — and being

Harassed by the ringing phone only to
Listen to recorded messages of
No interest to me — and encountering
Error after error in essays that

Require exacting correction while
Needing to finish quickly — and driving
Across town in haste but following a
Succession of the ambling elderly —

It seems I'm fighting a persisting wind
And each movement is testing my patience.

Calm attentiveness
gives way and my
hands express the
jitters.

I light the candle in the chapel that
Serves as our Zendo and we remove the
Extra chairs and carry and place the mats
And the cushions upon which we will sit

And the various bells are arranged in
Position — and before we begin there
Is conversation in the vestibule
And on some mornings I am a part of

The conversation and at other times
I am apart from the group listening
But not conversing — being one of the
Group being shaped by them and shaping them

By the expression of myself is why
My practice is so unpredictable.

Tension between
cooperation
separation
meditation
is a practice.

After a lifetime of cardio and
Weightlifting exercise probably I
Will live to be a hundred years old but
I am not sure that's entirely good

Because I could outlive all of my friends
And I haven't got as much money in
The bank as the retirement gurus
On T.V. say is necessary and

Who will pal around with a forgetful
And deaf and wrinkled old fart even if
He uses one hundred pound dumbbells at
The gym — and I think my kids don't like me —

Negative thinking is very easy —
I have to exercise positivity.

I am asking a
wood-working friend
to make a plaque
that says —
"It won't happen like that."

The cold returned to the valley and the
Ice on the river is deepening and
The air is biting the cheeks of my face
And the cold is sticking to folds of my

Jeans and my walking is painful but I'm
Grateful I can see the blue of the sky
And the impotent sun — and imagine
Being a catfish in the river with

The ice impeding the rays of the sun —
And the enveloping darkness and the
Impossibility of escaping
With the cold passing though its mouth and its

Gills — how could there be an expression of
Personality in the fish's eyes —

With the dull
harmony
of the cold
and the gloom?

Entropy is a scientific word
That means that systems consisting of
Organization and energy will
Over time break down and expire and

The effects of entropy are seen in
The eventual demise of the sun
And in the expansion and cooling of
The galaxies — and even the black holes

Where time does not exist are subject to
Entropy and they will also dissolve —
And I am grateful for the scientists
Who have extended the horizons of

Knowledge but they don't do much — while knowing
We will die — to show us how to live.

Scientists expend
energy learning
how things work but
meaning is an
afterthought.

I was driving east in Bayport towards the
River as I've done thousands of times in
Thirty years — down the hill to the corner
Of Main Street — and today I remembered

The first few days after my family
Moved our home from Hutchinson Kansas where
The land is as flat as a tabletop
To Bayport Minnesota that has hills —

And I recalled the thrill my brother and
I had coasting our bicycles down the
Hill with the wind in our faces and hair
When the little slope seemed like a mountain

Very hard to pedal up to the top
But such a joy to descend so quickly.

I wish it were
still possible to
be so easily
inspired with
simple novelty.

Considering rush hour traffic I
Left an hour before my appointment
So I didn't mind stopping at traffic
Lights but then I was surprised that the stop

And go traffic began so far from my
Destination and I saw the constant
Stream of cars on the ramps feeding into
The highway and I let a cargo truck

With a greasy rear end into the lane
Before me obscuring my view and I
Began to sweat the minutes with each ramp
Feeding more cars in front of me while I

Knew how far there was to go and we crawled
To a stop within sight of my exit.

There were slower cars
in front of me all the way
to the parking lot
and I was a minute late
but I came on the wrong day.

How differently experience appears
From day to day when sometimes my thoughts and
Words are joyous in conversation with
A friend and then at other times I can't

Seem to bridge a gap between us — and I
Know how good it is to spark a thought in
A companion and together we can
Build momentum and enthusiasm

And we can compare perspectives and the
Banter and the laughter are healing and
Clarifying as we give each other
The gift of optimism — but there are

Other days when I become a turtle
And I let the world go on without me.

Lightheartedness
and gratitude
can be practiced
and cultivated.

There is the moment every morning when
I close my eyes and feel my face with
My fingers — as I am using soap and
Washing my face — that is a moment for

Reflection — and it isn't easy to
Step outside and take a good objective
Look at myself — and I discover how
I'm getting along with the people in

My life and where the frictions are and why
I am holding the attitudes that I
Am — and there is the usual thinking
In defense of me that serves to cover

A sense of woundedness that if I'm not
Careful is all that I will ever see.

There are people
I don't want to be with —
but I don't want them
punished or condemned
which is liberating.

A sweeping of snow advances over
The northern plains of America and
On the evening before its arrival
The forecasters are predicting a foot

Of snow followed quickly by a polar
Vortex bringing a degree of cold that
We haven't had for decades — I retrieve
My snowsuit and long underwear and my

Moon boots from storage — assuming that the
Predictions are wrong as they often are —
And it's hard to believe the pattern of
Minimal snow and mild temperatures

Will turn so suddenly so I'll sleep cozy
Waiting for the morning facts to emerge.

One day to another
circumstances are
different so
I'm grateful
the snow blower
works.

Sunlight on a morning when the cold is
Colder than thirty below zero is
As lively as any sunrise can be
And the cloudless sky is as open and

As blue as a mild day in June — but
The cold is bearing down upon the land
And the naked branches of the trees are
Motionless and steam is rising from the

Vents of homes and there is only so much
Words can do in description of the thing
Itself — the cold is an enveloping
Pressure burning and making my breathing

Labored — and when I reenter my home
The emergence of warmth is a relief.

Crows
encounter
cold flying
between
trees.

Now the cold is gone and there will be rain
This afternoon and fog is obscuring
The trees as they look like shadows in the
Mist — as I am leaving in my car I

See the apple trees by the driveway and
There are the innumerable crooked
Twigs and so many drops of water are
Hanging from the crooks — and I can't say that

The sights are beautiful this morning as
The streets are a mess with the melting brown
And salty slush that smears the sides of the
Cars and sticks to my boots but rather I

Would say that there are many glimpses of
Beauty visible any given day.

This is not the
thaw of spring as the
rain will turn to
ice as a cold front
returns tomorrow.

Rain after arctic cold is surprising
And in February there's a bitter
Aftermath as the rain will freeze
And we are left with a coating of ice

On the walkways and driveways and the streets
And for those on the congested highways
Into the city speed is dangerous
And accidents are inevitable —

At my Mom's house the driveway that I have
To clear slopes down to the house and when it's
Icy walking is precarious and
Several inches of snow is forecast so

I will either push a machine and slip
And fall or scrape with a shovel and fall.

Driving out of the garage
and up to the street
I must go fast — or
I'll be spinning my tires
on the icy slope.

When backing out of my driveway after
A day of falling snow I powered through
The fallen snow but got stuck at the road
Where the city plow had left a pile of

Snow — I shoveled once to clear my tires
But could only spin my tires — and I
Shoveled again and then broke out onto
The street and proceeded on my way — it's

Unusual to have a sheet of ice
Under a dumping of snow and when I'm
Clearing my driveway — and my mom's too — I
Could grumble at the circumstances — but

I remember how hard it is to move
Wet heavy snow at the point of melting.

Moving snow is
easier when it's colder
and maybe the snow
atop the ice will
provide leverage?

My Mom's driveway slopes down to the house and
Side by side there are two garages with
A wall to one side so the driveway is
Wide and the snow has to be moved away

From the wall — and the rotational shoot
Of the twenty-year-old snow blower is
Faulty and can only be relied on
To stay put in the forward direction —

So I have to blow across the driveway —
And the with ice under my feet I found
Blowing forward not too hard — but jerking
The machine back with one arm extended

And stepping sideways precariously
Without slipping on the ice was tricky.

It's good to know that
two feet and a snow blower
provide a little
more stability than just
two feet on a sheet of ice.

I moved my car out of my driveway so
That I could snow blow the driveway after
The snow finally stopped falling because
It was getting much colder and the wind

Would be picking up — and afterwards I
Got in the car and attempted a u-
Turn to return the car to the driveway —
But because the city plows hadn't come

The road was a mess and I got stuck and
Another car came along and wouldn't
Pass and waited — and I was flustered and
Bothered and got out to ask the driver

To pass but I was surprised and humbled —
My neighbor wanted to help push me out.

In a moment of
botherment a
hearty young girl
came in the dark
to get me home.

February snow is different from
March snow because the temperature is
Colder and the snow happens to be light
And fluffy in the cold — and I prefer

Moving snow even in the most bitter
Cold to having the snow blower clog with
The heavy melting snow of March because
The snow is hardest to shovel in March —

And the February snow blower at
My Mom's house — even with new spark plugs — is
Different from the November snow blower
Because in November the snow blower

Is frustratingly hard to start but in
February it roars with one hard yank.

I'm sure there are
mechanical reasons
for the difference but
I am clueless.

Writing poems is an oasis in
A day when I may sit at my desk and
Separate myself from being busy
And see if I may find a meaning that

Is worthy of a poem — and today
I am enthusiastic about my
Butter honey nut formula lotion
Even though I'm a manly kind of guy

Because I like the way it smells and how
It sooths my skin during the dry winter
Months — and I am practical and I know
That without the lotion my finger tips

Would crack at odd angles next to my nails
And that is an irritating nuisance.

When the container
is almost empty I will
twist off the end and —
like a Pooh Bear with honey —
finger for every last drop.

My friend returned from a business trip to
India and he remarked about a
Hindu master who while blindfolded could
Read my friend's email address and the phone

Numbers on a business card and my friend
Said that the masters see the world from a
Quantum point of view and some of them use
Their powers for good and some are evil

And I am sure the spiritual life of
India is a deep reality
But in February I do need the
Ability to turn my weariness

Into optimism as the snow is
Falling every day and piling higher.

In India
my friend was asked —
is the snow real?
can you hold a snowflake
in your palm and watch it melt?

A blizzard erases the horizon
And only immediate surroundings
Are visible and it is a proof of the
Power of the sun that even on a

Snowy morning anything can be seen —
I left my car in the garage because
It's likely to get stuck on the streets and
As I am trudging through the snow the fine

Grains of the snow are swirling around the
Wire rims of my glasses and they tickle
Me about my eyes with tiny touches
Of the cold and in order to take my

Short cut I have to climb a bank of the
Compacted snow that a plow left behind.

It is a white world
with a foot of snow cloaking
and bearing down the
branches of coniferous
pines looking so composed.

There will be an end to the snow poems
When the season turns and we are happy
But now we have indistinguishable
Days with grains of snow descending from a

White sky — and there are the daily parades
Of city snow plows slapping another
Pile to the side — and where is vibrancy
When white and shadow predominate — and

It's difficult to remember what I
Did yesterday from the day before or
From what I did last week as the routine
Of snow blower shovel rest repeats and

I suspect there must be something about
Me that enjoys wallowing in the gloom.

Cherry blossoms are
beautiful but
beauty is enhanced
by what comes
before.

A Chautauqua was an American
Gathering of people that was done a
Hundred years ago for entertainment
And story telling and encouragement

With people meeting face to face — but now
We use the Internet and millions of
Americans use Twitter to comment on
The current events — using no more than

Two hundred eighty letters or spaces —
And videos of confrontations will
Rise to prominence inspiring a
Rage with millions of enthusiasts who

Stab their enemies with daggers as they
Hide their identity in cyber space.

Creating
scapegoats is
easier when
guardians are
anonymous.

There is pathology broadcast by the
Mass media — whether in the game shows
Where the adults are reduced to shrieking
Children — in the news reporting on the

Daily violence and tragedies — or
In the political narratives when
Over time the politicians and the
Reporters and the pundits take both sides

Of the same issues and it becomes clear
The issue is not the issue but that
The acquisition and maintenance of
More and more power among a select

And closed group of elites is the issue
And the voters are manipulated.

People are angry
because disturbing
narratives are created to
produce manipulated
angry people.

Humans in masses are scary because
Of our squabbling and scapegoating and
Tribal instincts and tunnel vision — and
We are easily manipulated

And vulnerable to mass hypnosis —
And there are demons among us who are
Driving us like cattle to destruction
Assaulting the American system

Of the separation of powers with
Devilish tricks of demagogy
With such furious ingenuity
Practicing the arts of accusation —

Humans are volatile and dangerous
Capable of unthinking cruelty.

Political ads
broadcasting thirty seconds
of accusation
rely on fear and envy
to channel revenge.

Before words were written on parchment they
Were remembered and passed on by word of
Mouth — if they were important enough — and
Someone said we are what we think and all

That we are arises with our thoughts — with
Our thinking we make the world — and he said —
Speak or act with an impure mind and your
Troubles will follow you like a wheel that

Follows the ox that draws the cart — and he
Said — we are what we think — all that we
Are arises with our thoughts — with our thoughts
We make the world — speak or act with a pure

Mind and happiness will follow you as
Your shadow — and these are remembered words.

This is a saying
of the Buddha
written later
in the Dhammapada.

[Adapted from Thomas Byrom's translation]

Friends are good for showing me other ways
Of living and I know a busy guy
In retirement who enjoys nature
And photography with a window that

Opens to a lake and he has a bird
Feeder in easy sight of the window
And during winter while we are reading
Samples of our writings to each other

There are yellow belly sap suckers and
Nuthatches coming and going and he
Says that if you put up a bird feeder
The birds will come and yes the migrating

Humming birds will return — and who could think
Such delicate birds would be migrating?

Leisure isn't
having nothing to do
but being free
from aggravation —
and loving life.

Once in a while an eagle is skimming
A current of air and if I were a
Photographer with an adjustable
Lens I could bring the bird into focus

And follow its effortless patrolling
For prey and I would be on the hunt for
The capture of the perfect shot in an
Instant with the correct shutter speed and

The necessary quantity of light —
And then I trade places and imagine
The eagle's ability to see and
The terrible gripping power of its

Talons and the ripping use of its beak
And its life of hunger and satiety.

The contrails of a
barely visible jet are a
hint of hundreds
of separate lives moving
rapidly across the sky.

Some people are clever enough to have
Figured out that a million seconds is
Almost twelve days and a billion seconds
Amounts to about thirty-two years and

A trillion seconds is near thirty-two
Thousand years — and the Lascaux cave drawings
In France are seventeen thousand years old —
And to study the events of the Big

Bang scientists will slice a second — and
A million parts are called microseconds
A billion parts are called nanoseconds
And a trillion are called picoseconds —

And in the observable cosmos
Are untold trillions and trillions of stars.

Does any of this
information explain
life and consciousness
or put cruelty and
kindness in context?

It is said that inside a space the size
Of a trillionth of the period at
The end of a sonnet the cosmos popped
As hot as ten thousand trillion trillion

Degrees and for fourteen billion years it has
Been expanding and accelerating —
And the temperature of the cosmos
Now is three degrees and it is thought that

At some point the stars will flicker out and
The black holes will evaporate — and as
Long as there is mass the planets will
Orbit but when the temperature is

Absolute zero the molecules will
Dissolve and the particles dissipate.

Beyond the alpha
and the omega there is
no knowledge possible
but my beating heart
continues.

There was another blizzard yesterday
And I cleared both of the driveways twice
Because it's easier to pace the work
Than to have too much to move at the end

Of the day — and the difficulty is
The compacted pile the city plows leave
Across the entrance of the driveway that
Can only be removed in slices with

The snow blower — and overnight a thin
Layer of fluff descended giving me
A little more to do — with a shovel
I scraped around in a meandering

Pattern curving my path and avoiding
The repetition of the back and forth —

Circling
sashaying like
Napoleon
outwitting the
Austrians
and Russians.

It is true that a life of resentment
Of people and circumstances is a
Wasted life and it is not easy to
Recognize the habit of resenting

As a source of my unhappiness but
Another impending blizzard with the
Forecast temperature rising above
Freezing and therefore bringing sleet and the

Worst of heavy wet snow is presenting
The opportunity for practicing
Acceptance and for elevating snow
In February to the level of

A tragicomedy — and who is to
Blame except for a Doofus Deity.

From the window above
my Mom's driveway it appears
what I thought was a straight line
is more of an angle and
now there is more snow to move.

If there are consciousness particles that
Come from a consciousness field and if such
Particles are waving permeating
Everything that I am able to see

Maybe I should think of myself as a
Node of consciousness with a peculiar
Ability to make choices and to
Evolve or devolve depending on the

Quality of my choices — so when I
Am presented with another falling
Of snow that I have to move with a snow
Blower and shovel I could be fuming

And occupied with the injustice or
I could be shoveling and marveling.

Imagine the result
of thirty years of
unresolved resentments
piled one over
another.

For those of us who don't dress up for an
Office it's routine in winter to wear
Insulated and oversized moon boots
That rise to cover our ankles as the

Conditions in Minnesota are not
Conducive to a ballerina on
Tippy toes in slippers as we get used
To clomping and moving the snow — and we

Get weary in our plodding so I will
Bend enough to untie my boots at the
Top and might even loosen the laces
But it's hard to bend all the way over —

Using my toes as leverage behind
My heels I pull my feet out of my boots.

About the middle of
a snowy February
a what-the-hell
attitude creeps
over us.

The snow blown by a hard persisting wind
Into a drift is different than it was
Before the wind as it gives a crunchy
Reaction when I'm stepping on it — and

The remnants of the blizzards piling one
Over another through the season are
Not the same snows that they were when falling
From the sky as temperature and time

Are having a continuous effect —
As soon as the weather warms and the snow
Melts in the afternoon and freezes in
The evening a crust will emerge on the

Surface and the piles along the street will
Deform as the melting begins to bite.

After twenty years
of clearing the same driveways
with the same tools I
notice I'm not quite the same
collection of attitudes.

The point of meditation is to wake
Which is what we say to each other and
Which implies that there is a boundary
To cross without directions where to go

And now that I've become familiar with
My history and propensities and
Am aware of the chattering antics
Of my thought I want to penetrate my

Life and throw off body and mind and be
Enlightened by myriad things as a
Famous monk remarked centuries ago
But it's also said the desire for

Awakening can become a problem
Leaving a person with nowhere to stand.

I don't really know
how to be nowhere
as I am always
somewhere
thinking.

The Japanese position vermillion
Tori gates at the entrance to their shrines
And the gates are called the abode of birds
Because the birds will perch on them — they are

So simple being only two posts topped
By two beams — and they are said to mark the
Crossing from the mundane to the sacred —
And I have crossed without noticing a

Difference and smirked — but after thirty
Years I remember them and recognize
That every day I may transition from
The ordinary into the sacred

As long as I believe the transcending
Is possible and is worth the seeking.

Another snowfall needs
moving and the snow may be
a tori gate as
I leverage energy
over negativity.

I wouldn't want to live without being
One of a group that delights in meeting
Each other where there is no striving for
Preeminence or authority to

Reduce our companions to a lesser
Status — and in my group we take turns in
Sharing the attention and every one
Turns to face the speaker and the practice

Of listening and responding in turn
Reveals that my concatenation of
Thinking is not unique to me but in
Fact my friends often share my patterns of

Thought — and the differences that emerge
Serve to show the way to innovation.

I heard about grabbing
the rear bumper of a
vehicle and about sliding
while trying to stay standing —
called hookybobbin.

Alcoholics are like pennies with one
Side showing miserable and lonely
Individuals on the way to a
Demise — but on the other side we are

Joyous and free as we learn to break the
Walls of isolation through sincere and
Patient communication — as we learn
To listen more than we did before — now

We rely on something we can't see or
Touch except when it emerges in the
Words of our fellow alcoholics and
The circumstances of our lives — and it

Becomes easier to trust no matter
What happens gratitude is possible.

Resentment
cherished long
enough leads
to my
demise.

To begin the discussion sometimes we
Read from a text — and I have heard the words
A gazillion times — and I like to read
To show off my articulation — and

I don't know if people are listening
Because they have heard the same words also —
But I plow ahead because there are sure
To be a few words that initiate

A conversation — I will be flowing
Pronouncing expertly while I'm thinking
About the snow and having to move it
Or I'm yearning for a lovely movie

Star — as the profundity of the words
And the meaning escapes my attention.

I can always
appear attentive
by expanding on
several ideas
within the text.

As I am dealing with the mess of a
Snowfall and subject to the timing of
The city snowplows I have often thought
About what it's like to be driving such

A forceful machine slapping the snow
To the side no matter how heavy and
Wet the snow may be — as I imagine
Myself a captain of the city streets —

And as a lowly owner of a home I
Am dependent on the plows to finish
With the snowfall and I must wait until
Their final pass that leaves the hardest and

Highest pile of compacted snow that takes
The utmost effort to shove to the side.

I resent the ease
with which they clog
my driveway — and
dislike that they always
get to my street last.

From my office there is a hill at the
Corner where I take a right turn and in
The middle of a blizzard before the
Plows clear the way there is no chance to build

Momentum up the hill and I have to
Judge whether it's possible to ascend
The slippery slope — and I was half way
Up but my tires were spinning without grip —

So I backed to the corner and turned down
A steeper slope towards a much higher hill
But because I picked up enough speed I
Barely made it to the top — and then I

Turned up a little hill without the push
I needed and almost got stuck again.

To get home I need
to guess the viscosity
of compressed snow and
fluffiness is a problem
but there's grip in heavy snow.

At my spot on the earth we have the March
Sun that is bright early in the morning
But the temperature is zero which
Is darn cold for humans — and I know that

Our sun and planets are moving as a
Unit orbiting in the Milky Way —
And I know the Milky Way is also
Moving together as a unit and

Expanding from where the Big bang happened
Along with all the other hundreds of
Billions of galaxies — and though events
Seem to happen gradually on earth

The earth is orbiting in the Milky
Way at five hundred thousand miles per hour.

The blue sky of morning
is concealing so much
of our reality
as I am sitting
quietly in a chair.

It is a bubble of a thought that burst
A moment before its proper time or
You could say it's a hiccup or even
An interruption of a really good

Inspiration that led to something quite
A bit better than itself later on
But as it is doesn't cohere into
A complete package that elicits a

Sense of satisfaction — as it looks like
A compendium of nonsensical
Elements that are fine enough if they
Were separate but together they are

Ridiculous — so I have to remark
Who could imagine the platypus?

And yet it swims
gracefully and waddles
along on land — and lays
its eggs and deploys
venom and growls.

It is a morning unlike the mornings
Of the previous weeks as I sit at
My desk and look out the window at the
Blue sky because today I have to put

On my wide brim hat to shield my eyes from
The emanations of the sun — and I
Enjoy absorbing the sunlight shining
On the piled snow seeing the pin-point jewels

Where the light is refracting into blues
And greens and reds in the snow that is just
Outside my window — and I am weary
Of so many overcast and snowy

Days and now it is a joy that the sun
Is bright enough for me to shield my eyes.

March is the snowiest
month perhaps but
the blooms of tulips
apple blossoms and
roses are coming.

We came to a point where the dry food was
Not healthy anymore as it induced
A urinary blockage in Johnnie
And then Henry got kidney disease and

Needs wet food from now on and it's better
To include Kit in the routine but then
One of them would look at the dish and not
Eat so we mixed two flavors together

And that worked for a while but we needed
Further inducement so a blender is
Useful for making puree with milk or
Water added sometimes but we came to

A point whatever is tried one of them
Looks at the dish turns around and walks off.

I am a chef for
discriminating
felines who don't care
as much as I do
about nutrition.

The trees in winter are in a trance of
Sleeping with their roots well established in
The earth firmly holding in the barren
Season and weathering the howling wind

And in their stark nakedness they become
Almost invisible but they are a
Quiet presence when I notice them in
Sunlight reminding me of my yearning

For roots attaching strengthening myself
Knowing I grow or wither depending
On whether I have the energy and
The will to embrace the supposition

In the midst of the incomprehensible
Suffering there is also a meaning.

There is a call
to awake to the
possibility
of growth in the midst
of difficulty.

The snow has piled storm after storm until
At the end of the driveway the piles are
Higher than me — and when I see the piles
About town I'm prideful about how we

Do manage to push aside enormous amounts
Of snow every year and go about our
Business — with rainy days forecast this week
I wonder whether the season turned and

Whether this is the week the snow begins
Irreversibly to pool on the streets
And flow downhill to the river — even
Though there may be snowy days ahead the

Preponderance of winter is over
And the sun will be reviving the earth.

Regardless of seasons
my hot water heater
provides enveloping
cascading warmth
every morning
shower.

The earth is cloaked in deep layers of snow
And walking between the piles I can feel
The cold emanating from the snow as
A persisting force that necessitates

The wearing of my warmest clothes and for
A thinner guy the cold penetrates and
I've left my neck and hands exposed with the
Intention of feeling the cold because

I am acclimated to the cold and
Even proud to be an inhabitant
Of the desolate northern plains hardy
Enough to be here as it isn't really

The weather that's the difficulty but
My wariness of people is what's hard.

Articulating my
occasional sense
of isolation among
people isn't easy —
the cold is easier.

Michelangelo was fired with a
Conception of God surrounded by his
Angels in heaven reaching out with his
Index finger to touch the finger of

Adam on Earth and perhaps in the act
Of touching God communicated a
Spark of divinity and a freedom
Of choice allowing for a growth into

The humane or for a dissipation
Into evil — and by the Renaissance
In Italy evil was already
Old in the world and people needed their

Consolations and inspirations and
We really aren't much different today.

Did Adam feel like
I did when opening
a tin of cat food
and slicing the tip of
my index finger?

A cloud has descended in Stillwater —
The homes and trees are emerging
Momentarily as I am driving —
Headlights are lighting the mist — the tires

Are splashing in the pools of the water
Collecting in the low places of the
Worn streets — as the accumulation of
Snow has peaked and the melting has begun —

The water is rippling and rushing
Across the many streets of Stillwater —
Down to the river — as the momentum
Of the days are evolving and snow may

Be possible yet — but I am feeling
The boisterous buoyancy coming with spring.

The sun
by itself in
the sky
will have
potency.

It takes practice to be spontaneous
As I am often taken by an urge
To argue a point of politics or
A voluptuous woman appears and

My pulse quickens — I have ammunition
To advance a case and I posses the
Qualities to make a favorable
Impression but it's not so easy to

Seize the moment and a second is just
Enough for hesitation to emerge —
I balance hope and defiance — passion
And carelessness — and just like faith and doubt

Produce good practice — excitement and poise
Can be joyously unpredictable.

Nothing is more
intoxicating
than clarity and
adrenalin.

There is rhythm to a day beginning
Before sunrise and the art of living
Usefully for me is learning how to
Harmonize my energy and relax

And when the sun rises I can see it
Through my window and I welcome the light
As if today were a day of boundless
Possibility and I were a child

But then there are responsibilities
And so many details and events that
Need attention and something will happen
That demands an extemporaneous

Response and I find myself in traffic
And everyone is driving too slowly.

A letter from
the Internal Revenue
Service is threatening
to seize my assets and I
need to see my accountant.

Getting a letter from the I.R.S.
Distorts the rhythm of a day as the
Threatening words are easy to see but
It's perplexing and excruciating

To decipher what the problem is — and
Last year my accountant untangled a
Mistake that the agency made but it
Seems different agents are repeating

The same mistake again — and another
Letter will have to be sent and I will
Have to navigate through their telephone
System and wait for an hour before

I reach an agent to persuade her to
Stop the impending seizure of assets.

While I was waiting
on the phone a
little red squirrel
scampered about the hedge
outside my window.

The melting of the snow progresses at
A gradual pace as there are cooler
And warmer days — and the piles along the
Streets that the city plows have left are the

Last to melt and I see the same houses
And bushes and the trees that are always
There as I'm driving and I am happy
The snow is disappearing as the snow

Is grimy and crusty and there are leaves
And tulips and apple blossoms to look
Forward to and — kerunk — a hole in the
Street jarred my tire and back and dang it

It's easy to daydream while driving and
I really hate hitting potholes in spring.

Dang it
a pothole
what the hell
was I thinking?

It can't be seen by only looking at
A person but once the conversation
Begins and honest words are exchanged then
I can see the battered appearance and

I can sense the depth of sincerity
In the selection of words and in the
Quiet and measured pace of expression
And then I know here is a kind and a

Well meaning person who has suffered and
Has determined to use intelligence
And experience and whatever pride
There might have been is washed away and now

There is a poise and a readiness to
Respond with a wealth of humility.

There is a sweetness
that only arises
from suffering and
a determination
to be helpful.

I was awake yesterday morning at
This time but I went to sleep later than
Usual and today my nose tickles
And there's fluid sloshing in my nasal

Cavities on the verge of eruption
And my eyes are dry and irritated
And I should be enthusiastic and
Energetic by now but instead there

Is the urge to go back to bed and I
Can't go back to bed and need to be as
Productive as possible — and last night
I read the words of a scientist who

Was considering the present moment
Writing it's hard to define what it is.

A squirrel is
climbing the branches
of a maple tree and
I coughed
three times.

A city takes on an identity
By the events that happen within it
And Chicago isn't recognized for
The transparency and honesty of

Its government so I wonder what the
Artist intended in placing The Bean
In a central plaza of the city —
And as a stainless steel sculpture curving

Like a bean it perfectly reflects the
Clouds and the artistic skyscrapers and
The many people who have the leisure
To enjoy it — and perhaps there is no

Cynicism implicit in it and
We are simply meant to savor the clouds.

I should dispense
with cynicism
and enjoy the
simplicity
and beauty.

The sound of the rain falling on the roof
At the beginning of the morning is
Peaceful and it isn't the first shower
Of the season but it is a soaking

Of the earth and a revival of the
Trees and bushes that have been dormant for
The long winter months and the air is damp
And the rain is spattering the puddles

On my driveway and the sky from which the
Drops are falling is misty and perhaps
The water will seep into my basement
And I'm prepared for excess water and

The gentle bombardment of the drops of
Rain will usher in a resurrection.

Each little drop
striking the earth
being absorbed
is one little touch
of revival.

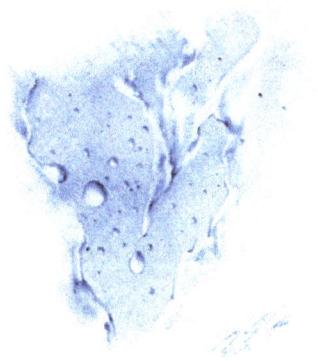

Brown grass and leaves on the ground left over
From fall are revealed on a sunny
Day and the branches are bare and without
The buds that will be coming soon — and the

Few clouds are transparent and are high in
The sky — and the clouds transforming from day
To day are not the things a person would
Notice as they are taken for granted

Like the grass the leaves the sun and the moon —
But the permutations of the earth are
Embedded in me — and as I'm getting
Better at quieting the clamor of

Fearful thoughts I am more likely to see
And rejoice with snowy egrets flying.

The ground is
sodden with
yesterday's
rain and is
preparing
miracles.

Sleep when it comes is a gift as I can
Forget about the troublesome details
Taking up my time and there is the drift
Into slumber and the waking early

In the morning and how well I manage
To sleep depends upon the amount of
Fear I carry in my days and depends
Upon whether I am seeing the things

That are flexible from the things that aren't
And whether I turn my fears over to
An invisible and untouchable
Power and on whether no matter what

Happens and even if I die I do
Believe in waking as if from a dream.

Dozing on my feet
or in my chair in
the afternoon is
what I do when not
managing well.

If I don't get moving in the morning
And don't feed and brush the cats and change the
Water in their dishes then I've giving
My mind the opportunity to think

About how lonely I am and how hard it is
To meet a girl while everyone else seems
To be happy — or I will ruminate
About the difficulties of making

Money — so I have to get up early
And do chores and meet my fellow sober
Alcoholics — and I have to practice
Turning from negativity to the

Positive and as long as I'm talking
With my friends it's easy to be joyous.

I make nonsense
noises or sing when
brushing and feeding
the cats — which
they expect.

I am ensconced in my neighborhood and
Once the piles of snow have vanished from the
Borders of my yard along the street I
Notice the gargantuan heaps in the

Parking lots and when they expire — as
They are on the verge of expiration
Now — I rejoice because the dreary months
Of winter are over but the sky is

Leaden the temperature is freezing
And people are mouthing the word snow and
The trees are moving with a bitter wind
Without their buds and I am questioning

Is today an April morning or a
Twilight resurrection of November?

This is a trick
weathered
Minnesotans
should expect
by now.

I am holding my two thermoses of
Coffee in my mittens while stepping through
A foot of snow on my way from home to
My office — which is what I do when it's

Not a good idea to take the car
From the garage because it's likely to
Get stuck on the street within sight of my
Home — and that would be a nuisance — so I'll

Sit on my chair and drink coffee and look
Out the window at the blowing snow and
At the branches of trees swaying in the
Wind and rejoice that on days like today

We can be within warm homes — and how did
People in the past manage to survive?

From the basement
I retrieved the one
piece snow suit and
the big boots that
almost reach my knees.

The first ever photo of a black hole
That is fifty-five million light years off
Was made by synchronizing atomic
Clocks and by focusing eight radio

Telescopes on several continents — thus
Making the earth a telescope — and by
Waiting for the moment when the weather
Was clear in Spain and Antarctica and

Chile — and the image shows a glowing
Doughnut with the edge nearest to the earth
Appearing brighter than the further side —
And the scientists deduce the burning

Ring is composed of the dust and gas flung
Around the hole and instantly consumed.

The cosmic
sinkhole
trapdoor
collapses
time.

Albert Einstein deduced the existence
Of black holes but before the photo was
Taken today no one had seen them and
To produce the photo astronomers

And physicists and mathematicians
And engineers combined their efforts — an
Algorithm was fashioned to remove
The atmospheric humidity of

The earth — and the scientists say that the
Extremity of the bending of light
Is such that if one sat on the edge of
The event horizon one could see the

Back of one's own head — a curious and
A puzzling statement that's hard to grasp.

With a celestial body
I would like to sit on the
edge of the event
horizon with a cane pole
and fish for mysteries.

If I didn't have to move the snow and
If it weren't so dangerous and messy
To drive about it would be a pleasure
To watch all the little differences

That snow manifests — it is falling in
Fine grains and slanting and curving about
Today and when a grain touches my face
There's a tiny tap of moisture on my

Cheek — and nature doesn't care about my
Temperament and I have to adapt to
Circumstances and it's natural for
A person on the earth to struggle to

Keep body and soul harmonious
While attending to the details of life.

Were the blue skies
and the reviving
landscape days ago
a dream — because today
looks like February.

I have a simple conception of sight
About the ability to see things
That I'm looking at — but the people in
Australia are walking about up side

Down and a scientist says that space is
Composed of interlocking rings that are
Billions and billions of times smaller than
An atom — and a physicist says that

Gravity operates upon mass and
Crushes every large object into a
Sphere and even though Mount Everest seems
Imposing — from an astronomer's view —

The earth would feel as smooth as a cue ball —
If I possessed gargantuan fingers.

What about a
consciousness
embodying this
cosmos and interlocking
cosmoses?

A couple of sparrows are content to
Sit on the branches at the top of the
Maple while the chickadees are diving
And flitting about and hopping in the

Bush outside my window — and the snow on
The bush melted yesterday into a
Dribbling that froze over night into
Such delicate icicles — and drops are

Forming from the icicles this morning
And falling — the chickadees are turning
Their heads and hopping a foot away from
Me in the bush with quick little movements —

The birds aren't bothered by the overcast
Sky or by snow on the ground and the roofs.

The white sky
is glowing
brilliantly
from sunlight.

Do you have those Saturday afternoons
When you don't know what to do with yourself
When the usual routine is to go
To the gym and grocery shopping but

This Saturday you just don't want to go
Because there's the intuition that life
Has so much more to offer but somehow
You've allowed yourself to get pigeonholed —

And the workweek is over and there was
No thought of behaving differently
Until the prospect of pumping iron
Again begets a undeniable

Revulsion making you paralyzed in
The parking lot wondering what to do?

Thank God for
ennui — I'd be
repetitive and
boring without
it.

What made the cat who was destined to be
Named Johnnie attractive to me in the
Animal shelter was his jump onto
My lap — his curling up and his purring —

Fifteen years later his urinary
Tract became infected and from then on
He needs expensive prescription canned food
And he waits to be fed four times a day

And for the last several years my home is
Transformed by the insistent yowling of
Johnnie begging to be fed when I come
In the door or periodically in

The day and he won't be quiet and all
I can do is learn to ignore the noise.

The affectionate cat
re-emerges sometimes
between bouts of
unquenchable
appetite.

Wolfgang Pauli noticed that a minute
Amount of energy was missing from
His equations so he postulated —
And has been proved correct — the existence

Of the neutrino — a subatomic
Particle with zero mass and without
An electric charge — that originates
From the continuing fusion within stars —

And at the speed of light the cosmos is
Penetrated with neutrinos that pass
Through the densest matter including the
Earth and humans with no discernable

Effect and scientists are wondering
Do they oscillate? Are they dark matter?

Which makes me
speculate what else is
penetrating me
constantly?

We would be better off if all of us
Were much more skeptical of what we read
In newspapers because journalism
Breeds cynicism and tribal thinking —

Which doesn't mean that journalists are not
Necessary to free societies —
But journalists cater to the masses
And bitterness and accusation make

Attractive headlines — it is difficult
To erase a negative portrayal
Of a person's reputation once the
News is circulated — and journalists

Escape the scrutiny that they deserve
By directing the attention elsewhere.

Power
and deceit
cooperate
like a hand
in a glove.

It is difficult to believe that each
Of us has a destiny that is an
Appointed destination that we can
Realize only after making the

Necessary decisions — coming as
We do from parents who came from parents
Who each carried stories about themselves —
As the stories are forgotten with the

Passing generations — and who can say
How much depends upon the mixing of
Personalities and dispositions —
As stories never tell the whole story —

Perhaps it's better not to think too much
Or to value — destiny — very much.

Destinies are made
in retrospect by
making connections
that maybe were true
and maybe not.

The trick about writing poetry is
Not to become too enamored of a
Word or a line too early — I don't have
To know what the ending will be and I

Don't have to have clarity from the start —
The playing with words is fun if I am
Willing to throw away what doesn't work
Because I know with practice a meaning

Will emerge and the meaning takes form as
Suitable words come to mind and the run
Of syllables and the mixture of the
Vowels and consonants find harmony

As I am hunting for illustrations
For how the world works — without illusions.

False starts are
frustrating
but patience
finds
satisfaction.

I'll break the rules of poetry with glee
And write a poem without images
Propounding only words and ideas
Raising a windstorm with consonants and

Vowels — and because meaning is vital
To me and is the most elemental
Ingredient of a human life I
Will winnow away the decorous in

Favor of significance — because
The world is like the bare branches with buds
And without a celebration of the
Budding of spring what would be the point of

Living a human life — and I want to be
Resonant like the wind passing in leaves.

I want to
write the right
words in a
proper order without
wasting a syllable.

A week ago the snow returned at a
Seeming tipping point and retarded the
Arrival of spring — but today the ground
Is clear again and the grass is greening

And I was frustrated and the people
I talked to were soured by the turn the
Weather took because it's been a long and
Snowy winter and we yearn for warmth but

The river is free of ice and didn't
Flood the downtown businesses as was feared
And we realize that resplendent days
Are on the way and the couple rainy

Days we had are normal in April and
I really didn't have to shovel the rain.

When the
impending
snowstorm
passed my
mood lightened.

I am leveraging as much morning
Energy as possible to open
My eyes and ears so that I inhabit
My living in cooperation with

The rising sun and what's noticeable
Is the spontaneity of waking
Again with an optimism that makes
Light of my burdens and cherishes the

Freedom to sing nonsense to my cats as
I'm brushing them — and there is no human
Sense in the singing but lightheartedness
And daily renewal carry impact —

I believe my cats know what to expect
And brushing and singing make me happy.

For much of my
living waking again
was a regurgitation
of burdens.

There comes a day every spring when I hear
Birdsong again with the rising sun and
I have no certainty about exactly
On which day the joyful creatures arrived

From their seasonal migration as the
Air is chilly and damp and I keep my
Windows shuttered until the warmth is well
Established — in the morning I hear the

Birds again responding to the sunrise
And marvel that such delicate creatures
Can transition through the air and return
To a familiar location and I

Admire their propensity to see
The sun rising up and to celebrate.

The birds remind
me of the beauty
and the mystery of
the earth beyond
comprehension.

There once was a woman named Jill
Who lived on a prominent hill
She was famous in town
For fooling around
And for making an ass out of Bill.

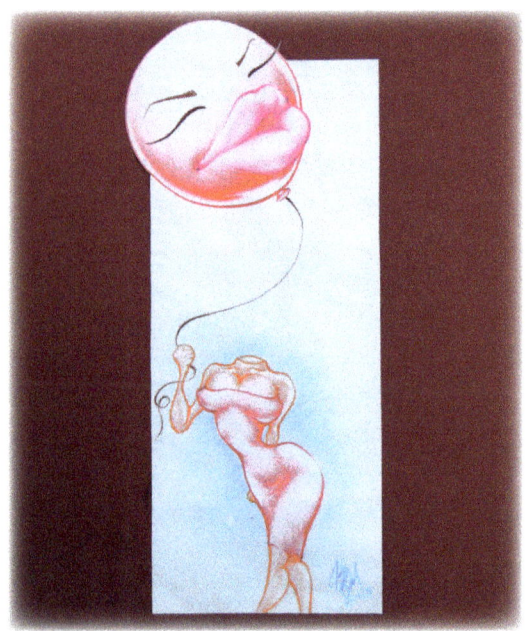

The speaker was passionate about the
Night he was camping above the tree line
In the Sierra Mountains and waking
Under the moonlight and absorbing the

Panorama of the mountains and the
Canyons and feeling the significance
Of his life diminish to nothingness —
And he felt himself dying but then an

Answering response arose that in his
Smallness he is a part of the cosmos
And before and afterwards disappeared
And there was only presence and though the

Experience happened years ago he
Has been transformed ever since that night.

The experience was
unbidden and however
much desired it can't
be gained by
force of will.

I dropped in the beef stew meat and emptied
The cans of stewed tomatoes green beans and
Kernels of corn — and then I cut mushrooms
Cauliflower broccoli and onions

Into appropriate pieces and put
Them into the crock pot — it's curious
To me that very much foodstuff can go
In the slow cooker and yet there is room

For plenty of water — I calculate
The amount of chicken powder needed
Knowing it's easy to add some later
But I'm tempted to use a lot at once —

Last Sunday morning I used too many
Mushrooms and forgot about the onions.

On returning home
outside of my door
of all the ingredients
I smelled green beans
and broccoli.

Transitions

Before the assassinations of the
Kennedy brothers and Martin Luther
King and before the Tet Offensive there
Was the Beatles Revolution and the

Intoxication of rhythm and blues
And the generation older than me —
While I was self-conscious and clumsy and
Awakening to loneliness and desire —

Grabbed me by the balls — and breasts and lips and
Long hair and visions of ecstasy in
San Francisco took me over and I
Listened to music on the radio

And wanted romance and liberation
And I was ashamed of my family.

My Dad the
Congregational
minister once
a month
hacked
my hair
short.

There was a sharp edge to my Dad as he
Condemned so many people and so much
Of popular culture and now I know
That he saw himself as a failure which

Exacerbated the vehemence of
Of his opinions — as he immigrated to
America from Australia as
A youthful Christian minster who loved

Classical music and who aspired
To be scholarly and inspirational
But instead he encountered persisting
Opposition and indifference and

He hungered for appreciation but
Serious ambition is dangerous.

He was a little
fellow in a very large
country and people
were misdirected and he
couldn't change anything.

I remember listening to my Dad
As he was driving and I was sitting
Beside him and he stressed the importance
Of having a philosophy of life

Which meant discovering reasonable
Explanations that can only be done
By absorbing the intelligence of the
Most brilliant people who wrote histories

And philosophies — and to find the truth
Meant sorting through the centuries of thought
And learning to distinguish between that
Which is formidable and diseased

And that which is penetrating and honest —
As only the very best are humane.

His vehemence was
off-putting and as
an introverted
adolescent I
only wanted friends.

I understood my Dad well enough to
Respect his ideals and I admired
His courage and ambition when he quit
The church and established a journal of

Opinion but I also resented
Having to grow up with controversy
And partisanship and I divided
Myself from America by living

In Japan for almost a decade and
By becoming a Buddhist and taking
Up a quest for enlightenment and I
Wholeheartedly believe Americans

Put too much faith in ideology
Even in vicious ideologies.

Today hindered by
worldly attachments
I'm practicing to
dispense with body and
mind and be liberated.

The decades pass quickly and opinions
Are like the clouds that are similar from
Day to day and I practice naming my
Emotions and when I am angry or

Afraid or indulging in self-pity
It becomes easier over time to
Let my emotions go and I can choose
Whether to be unhappy or to see

The miracle of a sunrise on a
Frosty morning or to take note of the
Different manifestations of snow
Or to enjoy the return of robins

And when snow on the ground is melting
The afternoon warmth is marvelous.

I brought a wife and
children from Japan
to live in America
and I began working
with my Dad.

The Buddha began a tradition of
Leaving home and seeking enlightenment
And I left America and returned
To America with a family

And I worked with my Dad dabbling with
Opinions and politics and playing
With words believing it might be helpful
To mix Western and Eastern ideas

And much of my time is dedicated
To impartial justice and liberty
Because I understand that if freedom
Isn't defended tyrants will arise

And I also believe that greed anger
And ignorance are consuming poisons.

Before he died
Dad struggled and
mumbled to me
"I trust you to
keep me alive."

The dust is gathering on the books of
The shelves and some are books I've collected
But hundreds belonged to my Dad and there
Are the writings of Aristotle and

Bacon and the Common Book of Prayer and
Machiavelli and they are precious
With wisdom — and there are political
Books that time has rendered meaningless and

The paperback Westerns and detective
Adventures that diverted my Dad from
More serious reading — and in any
Of these thousands of bound pages I am

Likely to encounter the notes he wrote
In the margins revealing his presence.

The words are there
to read and consider
but I haven't the time
or inclination to
follow him.

The conversation happened thirty years
Ago and I don't recall what he said
Before or afterwards but I cherish
The words Zen Master Harada spoke to

Me as he said you need to trust yourself
And he cut across the differences
Of cultures and he appeared as solid
And settled as a mountain and the words

Are puzzling and without context but
Meaning emerges with the years that I
Needn't live in the oppositional
World where people struggle for attention —

Wholehearted effort is important and
There is a path opening before me.

A house is
commodious
in winter but
I want to be
at home anywhere.

Dad's
personality is
dispersed in
books
editorials
memory
words.

Snap Shots

I hold my possessions and remember
The memories they convey — and they are
A physical reality but they
Are also associated with a

Vanished world — my ex-wife is Japanese
And she has a shoebox of photos that
Were taken by her grandfather who was
A photographer with a platoon of

The Japanese Imperial Army
As he recorded the subjugation
Of China — my daughter began drawing
In grade school and she selected from the

Shoebox a tiny photo and drew a
Curious approximation of life.

I marvel at
the composure of
the Chinese man
seeing the
invaders.

The art colleges of America
Invite aspiring high school students
To an art fair in Minneapolis —
And in February of their senior

Year the students bring their artwork to show
The representatives from colleges — and
The parents and the students come to see
The quality of the art on offer —

And to see the representation of
The schools and to sample the various
Programs — and there is competition and
Nervousness among the students as if

Their worthiness depended completely
On the approval of their creations.

Jittery students
waiting in line and
glancing at the
competition are
busy comparing.

The pert voluptuous women and the
Dandy young men from the art colleges
Put on an exalted appearance as
They consider the line of supplicants

And they make suggestions for improvements
And they explain the advantages of
Their schools — and they take names and record their
Impressions of the encounters — and they

Don't really believe the pencil drawings
Done from photographs to be real artwork
Because the drawings are not creations
But are only copies of photos and

The authentic works of art must involve
Cultivated conceptual aplomb.

For years Jocelyn
was winning teenage
contests at county
and state fairs with
drawings of photos.

The fair was exciting and exhausting
And Jocelyn was torn between schools in
Alberta and Philadelphia but
Eventually she indulged her dream

And chose Moore College of Art and Design —
Not accounting for years of ensuing
Debt and the difficulty of finding
Employment after college — she painted

Portraits of models and fashioned a life-
Sized self-portrait in wire mesh and with an
An enormous canvas painted herself
Again using her feet — and it looks like

Brush work — and within a year in Philly
She met her future fiancé Eric.

Eric's a native
Philadelphian
and knows the gritty
metropolis.

We are the present manifestation
Of what came before us even if we
Don't know what happened before we came
Along and so we can't really gage how

Lucky or unfortunate we are — but
We can learn to see the landmarks on our
Way and become sensitive to the
Importance of being kind — even when

It's easy to get angry — my Dad was
An immigrant from Australia and I
Brought back a wife from Japan and now
Jocelyn is engaged to Eric whose

Family comes from Puerto Rico and who
Knows what happened hundreds of years ago?

Just a moment of
anger can twist the
direction of the
present
unpredictably.

Jocelyn was able to study at
Moore College of Art and Design because
Her grandmother Rema had carefully
Saved enough money and because Rema

Was generous and loving enough to
Pay for a large portion of tuition —
And after graduation Jocelyn
Was fortunate to paint the face of the

Famous broadcaster Ed Bradley and
And lucky to paint the players of the
76-ers Basketball team — and
These murals will brighten the buildings of

Philadelphia for decades to come
As real evidence of accomplishment.

Mural artists aren't
paid well and others
take the credit for their work
so Philadelphia
became depressing.

Leaving the classroom and entering the
Work force is disruptive and departing
From Philadelphia with Eric when
The ebb and flow of income became too

Unmanageable and returning to
Stillwater Minnesota was a shock —
Because Jocelyn and Eric had to
Accept the jobs with modest salaries

And stay with grandmother Rema — until
They could find better jobs and save money
And buy a car and get an apartment —
And now Jocelyn is painting when she

Can and she's working at the nursing home
Where her grandfather Angus passed away.

Jocelyn is
working with her mother
Yoshiko at the
nursing home as life is
spiraling from the past.

Cover Art by Jocelyn MacDonald

As Jocelyn's Dad
I'm helping when I
can but mostly
I'm observing.

— *Tekkan*

www.ingramcontent.com/pod-product-compliance
Lightning Source LLC
Chambersburg PA
CBHW042117100526
44587CB00025B/4089